Reasons to Watch CNN

Bobby Smith

ISBN-13: 978-1548188177
ISBN-10: 1548188174

DEDICATION

This is dedicated to all of the loyal Trump supporters out there who stood by President Trump throughout the 2016 election campaign. We all want and deserve to have factual news coverage that doesn't have an agenda behind it. NO FAKE NEWS.

CONTENTS

ACKNOWLEDGMENTS

I would like to thank Sean Hannity, Tucker Carlson, and Jesse Watters at Fox News for your honest and reliable news coverage. You three are a breath of fresh air. Keep up the great work!

1 QUALITY

Bobby Smith

Reasons to Watch CNN

Bobby Smith

Reasons to Watch CNN

Bobby Smith

Reasons to Watch CNN

Bobby Smith

Reasons to Watch CNN

2 TRUSTWORTHINESS

Reasons to Watch CNN

Bobby Smith

Reasons to Watch CNN

Bobby Smith

Reasons to Watch CNN

Bobby Smith

Reasons to Watch CNN

3 EVIDENCE

Reasons to Watch CNN

Bobby Smith

Reasons to Watch CNN

Bobby Smith

Reasons to Watch CNN

Reasons to Watch CNN

Reasons to Watch CNN

4 INTERPRETATION

Reasons to Watch CNN

Bobby Smith

Reasons to Watch CNN

Reasons to Watch CNN

Bobby Smith

Reasons to Watch CNN

Bobby Smith

Reasons to Watch CNN

5 COMPLETENESS

Reasons to Watch CNN

Bobby Smith

Reasons to Watch CNN

Bobby Smith

Reasons to Watch CNN

Reasons to Watch CNN

6 KNOWLEDGE

Reasons to Watch CNN

Bobby Smith

Reasons to Watch CNN

Reasons to Watch CNN

Bobby Smith

Reasons to Watch CNN

7 SOURCES

Bobby Smith

ABOUT THE AUTHOR

The author of this book is not Bobby Smith. Bobby Smith is the name the author chose to use for anonymity reasons. The author chose to remain anonymous not out of fear but out of principle. One doesn't need glory or praise when they are simply trying to expose the flaws in the information you consume. The author's content has been seen by over 250 million people around the world. It is highly likely you have encountered their work before. Until next time.